Matthew 1
c.1200 – 12.
Monk, Chronicler, Map-n

Matthew Paris was a monk of the Benedictine Order who lived and worked in St Albans Abbey in the thirteenth century. He was a prolific writer and an artist with a distinctive style. From 1236 until his death in 1259 he produced well over a million words recording the events of his time and the history of the Abbey. The books he wrote still exist, kept safely in the British Library in London, and in libraries in Cambridge and Dublin. These manuscripts are profusely illustrated with pen and ink drawings picking out the most important events in Matthew's great historical narrative. His work is the source of much of our knowledge of the Middle Ages today, and gives us a fascinating insight of how one man, and the community of which he was part, viewed the world in which they lived and the events they lived through.

Who was Matthew Paris?

Unfortunately we know very little about Matthew, other than the occasional reference to himself in his writings and a few comments from other members of his community. We know nothing of his parents, his place of birth, his social background, nor even his nationality. He was known as Matthew Paris, which could indicate that he came from France and in particular from Paris where he might have attended the University. There were strong links between St Albans and Norman France: Paul de Caen, who re-established the Abbey in 1077, and several of his successors, came from Normandy; John de Cella, who was the abbot when Matthew first came to the Abbey, taught in Paris. Matthew took a great interest in French affairs and had contacts in France, but there is no evidence that Matthew was French.

So was he an Englishman? The use of Paris as a surname in England was not uncommon. Its frequency in documents relating to Lincolnshire has led some to suggest that Matthew might have come from that area. Again, there is no evidence. His Englishness has been inferred from the bias towards England found in some of his writings, although he is as deeply critical of the king of England and his counsellors as he is of the French. There is no evidence that he wrote English, even if he understood it.

What is known is that he became a monk at St Albans on the feast of St Agnes (21st January) in 1217. We know this because he tells us so in his Chronicle. How old he was at the time is not known. It is often assumed that he was 17 which was the earliest he could be admitted and clothed as a monk. He may have been older and lived in the community for some time before this. However old he was, he dedicated the rest of his life to the community there, and to St Alban, whose relics were the heart and soul of the Abbey.

Matthew's background and social standing

Nothing definite is known about Matthew's background and social standing. From his writings and an analysis of the sources of his information, we gather that he was at home with the highest in the land; he was known to King Henry III, close to the king's brother, Richard of Cornwall, and intimate with many of the king's counsellors as well as the ladies of the court. He was known to Louis IX, King of France and was entrusted with messages from him to Haakon, King of Norway.

This then was no ordinary, everyday monk. He wrote for the court, for an Anglo-Norman French speaking community, as well as his Benedictine brethren. He was self-confident with strong views, confronting those in authority with his words, whether king or counsellor, pope or bishop. Did he come from the nobility, an illegitimate son perhaps, and inherit his personality and abilities from such a background?

And yet, although Matthew had the contacts and was a noted writer, he never achieved high office in his community. Why was this? In a community numbering 100 monks there were undoubtedly others skilful in leadership and ambitious for advancement: Matthew seems to have accepted his role and made it distinctive by the quality and breadth of his output. He makes no comment, nor does he complain, about the role assigned to him. His predecessor, Roger of Wendover, had been both the Precentor in the Abbey and, subsequently, Prior of Belvoir, a daughter house in Leicestershire. Matthew held none of those positions. But he possessed practical as well as literary skills: he was praised by a later chronicler of the Abbey, Thomas Walsingham, not only as '*a magnificent historian and chronicler*', but also because '*he had such skill in the working of gold and silver and other metal, and in painting pictures*' that he had no equal. Matthew was valued as a writer and an artist, and, as those words written 150 years after his death imply, his reputation in his community, and more widely, remained consistently high.

Fig. 1: Portrait of Matthew Paris, from Thomas Walsingham, Catalogue of the Benefactors of St Albans Abbey.

Matthew's education

What sort of education might Matthew have received? How did he develop an ability to write fluent prose and verse in both Latin and Anglo-Norman French (sometimes called insular French or the French of England)? His style is not sophisticated, and the evidence for his reading points to an acquaintanceship with standard works rather than a radical engagement with the thinking of his day. He was, as the historian Richard Vaughan commented, more of a journalist than a theorist, picking up the latest news that was brought to the Abbey by its numerous visitors, and recording it in an engaging and compelling way. For that we can be thankful, because his inquisitive nature and instinct for a good story has left us with an incomparable record of the concerns of people in thirteenth century England. His education, however it took place, owed much to the culture of the Abbey community of his time. This was a place where people could develop their inherent abilities. Some got seriously distracted: Alexander of Langley, for example, had great literary skills but suffered an acute breakdown. The best, however, lived lives of great seriousness and distinction. Matthew comments on John de Cella (1195-1214), the twenty-first Abbot, that he was renowned for his learning in grammar, poetry and medicine. It was John de Cella who could recite the book of psalms backwards from memory! It was a world led by such men that enabled others, such as Matthew, to achieve their potential.

Matthew's achievements

So what did Matthew do, that we should hold him in such esteem? First and foremost he was the historian of the Abbey; as such he compiled five chronicles, six saints' lives, two local histories, and a collection of documents crucial to maintaining the Abbey's privileged status. In addition he produced numerous illustrations of the subject matter he wrote about, including 300 drawings of heraldic shields, and no less than 15 maps and diagrams. To gather the material that went into his writings Matthew attended many special events and important meetings of church and state in person, and made contact with people who could give trustworthy accounts of historical events in which they had taken part. He seems to have frequented the Court in London, and visited the Exchequer, where he had access to government records; he attended events in York and Winchester; and travelled to Norway to re-establish the Benedictine community at Nidarholm, a journey which also involved an audience with the King of Norway. When he was not travelling to gather information, he was developing a network of informants in the Abbey where he was in contact with a regular stream of visitors from around the world.

Matthew's Chronicles: The Origin of the Chronicle

Matthew Paris's *Chronica Majora* (Greater Chronicle) was one of many chronicles written in the twelfth and thirteenth centuries. Each chronicle was a record of the events which were considered significant to a particular religious community in any one year. The format for the chronicle derived from the time when the collective memory of a community was being transformed into a written record.

Early Christian communities wanted to recall significant events in their history, and did so by including them in their liturgical cycle. To achieve a more permanent record of local events it became customary for Christian communities to annotate their Easter Tables with a one line entry. As the oral tradition faded so the amount of information committed to writing grew, and the chronicle as Matthew knew it was born. The simplicity of an annal entry became a sophisticated narrative.

Most chronicles were the work of a named individual who often incorporated previous material. In the case of St Albans, Matthew identifies himself as the author of the *Chronica Majora.* However, it was not entirely Matthew's work as he used an existing work by Roger of Wendover to describe the events which occurred before his own lifetime. Roger, who was also a monk of St Albans, wrote an account of the history of England covering the period from Creation to 1235, known as *Flores Historiarum* (The Flowers of History). Roger died in 1236, and from 1236 until 1259 the St Albans' *Chronica Majora* is the work of Matthew alone.

The size of Matthew's achievement in writing his Chronicle is difficult to exaggerate. His contribution for the years 1236 to 1259, plus the documents in his appendix, amount to over 2300 pages in the printed edition. It is simply the most comprehensive chronicle produced in England in this period. As the historian V. H. Galbraith said, *'history on this scale in the medieval period is unique.'*

Matthew's intention in writing his Chronicle

Matthew Paris inherited Roger of Wendover's work, incorporating it into his own account, which was a common practice at the time, but he also expanded and elaborated it. Matthew originally intended to end his Chronicle in 1250 because he thought, as did many other people, that the world would end in that year. However, when nothing untoward happened Matthew continued writing until his death in 1259.

Matthew's purpose in undertaking his great enterprise is not very explicit. When he concluded his entry for 1250 he wrote *'Here end the chronicles of Brother Matthew Paris, monk of St Albans, which he has committed to writing for the benefit of posterity ... lest the memory of present-day events be destroyed by age or oblivion.'* In the preface to his Chronicle, in reply to criticism from his contemporaries regarding the value of writing chronicles, he wrote, *'Let them know that the good lives and virtuous manners of men of old time are recorded to serve as patterns for the imitation of subsequent ages.'*

Fig. 2: A page of Matthew's *Chronica Majora*.

Matthew draws a comparison between reading a chronicle and reading the Bible, saying that both teach us *'to fear and to love God.'* Clearly Matthew had a strong moral and didactic intention in composing his works, which may account for the often extreme judgements he makes on human behaviour, particularly on the behaviour of those who held high office.

Apart from the moral intention behind his work, we can detect other purposes in his writings. For example, he wanted to record the history of the Abbey to support the charters, writs and papal letters which were kept in the Abbey's muniments chest. They provided the evidence on which the privileges and status of the Abbey were founded. Both the charters and Matthew's Chronicle could be used to defend the Abbey's status in any legal action.

His written work was also a celebration of the living presence of St Alban in his shrine in the Abbey. Matthew regularly invoked Alban, to deter enemies and encourage supporters. The martyr's presence encouraged pilgrims to come to the shrine to offer gifts of land and money, which were essential for the maintenance of the community. Matthew was always keen to foster such gifts. Finally, Matthew believed he had a responsibility to promote the Abbey as a centre of Benedictine excellence and spirituality and to encourage the strict observance of Benedict's Rule. To achieve his intentions, it was essential to have a coherent account of the Abbey's history in chronicle form.

Matthew's written work: his topics

Matthew Paris was a prolific writer with a particular interest in the history of his time. Today there is no exact equivalent to the position he occupied in the Abbey. He has been compared to a journalist reporting the news, or a columnist commenting on the political and ecclesiastical scene. He was also something of an archivist collecting and copying official documents: papal, monastic, political and legal. The scope of his subject matter was extensive.

In his Chronicle Matthew records events in strict chronological order; as a result major events alternate with relatively minor incidents and accounts of miraculous happenings. Because of the way the Chronicle is structured there is no over-riding theme which unifies the work. People reading it for the first time comment on how fragmented it is. It is not like a novel with a particular story to tell, nor is it a tract with an argument to make. It is a patchwork of information about people and events: about the actions and aspirations of kings, churchmen and nobles; about the succession and death of notable people; about the natural world and unusual events; about storms and catastrophes, harvest and famine. Matthew makes no attempt to organise around themes or identify trends. Nevertheless, from the mass of material which he records, it is possible to pick out the dominant concerns and events of the twelfth and thirteenth centuries, and trace their impact on individuals and institutions.

One way to identify the dominant topics from five volumes of printed text is to use the index, which fills one whole volume. If we compare the entries there, we can get some idea which topics Matthew recorded most frequently. The deeds of England's kings were Matthew's major concern: references to Henry III occupy 81 columns in the index; King John, 20; Henry II, 12; and Richard the Lion Heart, 11. Six popes ruled the church during Matthew's lifetime resulting in a total of 53 columns of references: Innocent IV (1241 – 1254) achieving the most with 29. The Archbishops of Canterbury from St Augustine to Boniface of Savoy occupy 37 columns. St Albans, including its abbots, monks and burgesses, takes up 26 columns. Some individuals are regularly referred to: Frederick II, Holy Roman Emperor, occupies 22 columns; Louis IX, King of France, 17; Richard of Cornwall, Henry III's brother, 16; Simon de Montfort, Earl of Leicester, and leader of the rebellion in 1258, 5; William Marshal, third Earl of Pembroke, regent and protector of the young Henry III, 3 columns. Then there are dozens of brief references to the people, places and events, which make up the tapestry of the Chronicle account.

Fig. 3: Marriage of Emperor Frederick and Isabella of England, sister of Henry III.

The dominant topic is undoubtedly Matthew's commitment to England. It is the concept of England as a nation, of Englishness, and the cry of 'England for the English,' which resonates throughout Matthew's Chronicle, and gives it its distinctive, and somewhat xenophobic character. In a way Matthew documents the birth of the English nation in the post-Conquest world.

After King John lost control of Normandy and western France in 1204, kings, barons, churchmen and old families, who since the Norman Conquest had divided their loyalty between France and England, were forced to concentrate on their English possessions and build their power bases there. Matthew is caught up in this period of transition, and the tension associated with it, and describes it in vivid and passionate words.

In many ways he gets carried away with his commitment to England, judging people and events exclusively by the way they supported or ignored his concept of the national good. He was critical of King John, decried the weakness and profligacy of Henry III and had no sympathy with Henry's commitment to his continental possessions. He supported Magna Carta and the barons in their struggle to limit the power of the king. He regularly denounced the practices of the papal curia and insisted that the church in England was a national church whose resources should not be used to fund the lifestyle of the church in Rome.

Fig, 4: King John.

And yet he was not totally exclusive in his views. He took great interest in the success or otherwise of the Crusades; was impressed by Frederick II, and carefully recorded the progress of the dispute between Frederick and the papacy; he was worried by the Tartar and Mongol armies on the borders of Europe; and believed that the quality of the Benedictine life as practised in St Albans should be shared with similar communities on the continent.

Apart from his anguish at the state of the kingdom, another major concern for Matthew was the status and privileges of St Albans Abbey. He records the many occasions on which the Abbey tried to resist the power of the King to interfere in its life and tax its resources. The privileges of the Abbey derived from two sources: from charters issued by the king, and from formal papal letters known as bulls. Matthew copied both charters and papal bulls into his Chronicle, either into the main text or into an appendix which he called the Book of Additions.

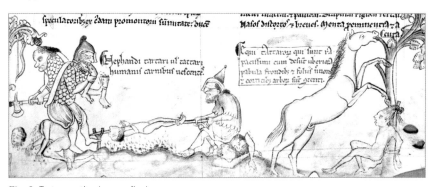

Fig, 5: Tartars eating human flesh.

Matthew records numerous occasions when privileges granted by the king in a royal charter were abused in some way. For example the Abbey was granted exclusive rights to hunting over land adjacent to the Abbey, but local landowners such as Geoffrey of Childwick deliberately ignored the Abbey's rights. The abbot complained to the king, but because Geoffrey was married to the sister of John Mansel, the king's chief counsellor, Geoffrey escaped censure. Matthew himself reproached the king about this on one of his visits to the Abbey. He records the conversation, and adds his own sceptical take on the king's reply: *'When the writer of this book, namely Brother Matthew Paris, undaunted, reproached the king over this affair, the king said, "Well, well, we will think about it". But the memory of these words and promises died away with their sound.'* Matthew's Chronicle was intended to support the abbot when he sought redress, and to encourage the community to pursue their rights, despite the influence of powerful individuals.

Fig, 6: Pope Adrian IV.

St Albans was fortunate that the only Englishman elected pope, Adrian IV (1154 – 1159), was associated with the Abbey, and favoured it by granting it extensive privileges in two bulls issued in 1156 and 1157. Apart from acknowledging the Abbey's exemption from a wide range of secular privileges, Adrian also exempted the Abbey from the jurisdiction of the diocesan bishop, who in this case was the Bishop of Lincoln. This meant that St Albans retained the tithes and income from all the manors and churches which had been granted to it over the years. This, together with the right to retain the fines imposed by the king's justices on men from the Liberty of St Albans, was an important source of income for the Abbey. However, although the privileges granted by the king or pope might benefit the Abbey, there were always people who were looking to reduce them; and the Abbey spent much time and energy ensuring that each succeeding king and pope confirmed and renewed the old privileges and extended them if possible. Matthew deliberately collected together all the written evidence he could find, and failing written evidence, the verbal accounts of reliable witnesses. Constant vigilance and careful record keeping was essential, and the Chronicle played a critical part in that process.

But it was not only the status and privileges of the Abbey that concerned Matthew. His commitment to the Benedictine ideal as set out in the Rule is also reflected in his Chronicle, where he stresses the importance of order, stability, and simplicity. His attitude towards the acquisition of power and wealth, and his condemnation of the cruelty, greed and extravagance associated with it, are all shaped by this commitment.

Nevertheless Matthew Paris was no ascetic. He appreciated beautiful things, as the illustrations in his manuscripts and his interest in the embellishment of the Abbey under William of Trumpington, demonstrated. When Matthew died he gave the Abbey the silk wall hangings he had been given by King Haakon of Norway and Queen Eleanor, King Henry's wife, a selection of silk vestments embroidered with gold, a number of sacred vessels in silver and his collection of books, some of which still exist   He was also financially astute, and in 1248, he was asked to sort out the finances and governance of the small Benedictine abbey of Nidarholm in Norway by the King of Norway and Pope Innocent IV.

Matthew's other great interest was in what we might call the dynastic politics of Europe: King John and Henry III's struggle to regain their possessions in France; the election of the Holy Roman Emperor; and the long conflict between the emperor and pope over who had ultimate power over the empire. Another of his interests was the progress of the Crusades. Gaining access to Jerusalem and the holy sites was a touchstone of Christian commitment. Matthew received lengthy letters and verbal accounts of the successes and failures of the various campaigns from visitors to the Abbey who had returned from the Crusades and from Richard of Cornwall who had led one of the Crusader armies. He recorded how possession of the Holy Land swung back and forth between the Crusader armies and the Saracens and the bravery, intrigue and exasperation resulting from the long struggle. In effect Matthew was the war correspondent for his community. But there was more to it than simply recording the information: for Matthew and his readers the words, and the act of reading them, were an expression of faith by those who could not make the sacrifice to join the Crusade. They could participate in the event by proxy.

Fig, 7: The siege of Damietta 1219.

Finally, in a world where the livelihoods of the population were dependent on agriculture, Matthew was acutely aware of the natural world and its vagaries. He comments on the weather and its effect on people and harvests throughout his Chronicle. In 1246, he describes *'a dreadful storm, attended by thunder and lightning, and also by hail, the stones of which were angular and most hard, the size of almonds, which destroyed birds and even some animals.'* In 1250, he recorded an earthquake which occurred in St Albans and the adjacent districts: *'a remarkable circumstance took place during the earthquake ... the pigeons, jackdaws, sparrows, and other birds, were seized with fright, and suddenly ... took to flight as if they were mad. This earthquake struck terror into the hearts of all.'* In 1258 a terrible famine occurred in England, after months of rain. Many thousands died or were made destitute. Shipments of corn and bread were sent from Germany and Holland. Matthew says, *'In some places, indeed, although late, and the crop of little use, it was cut and carried, whilst in many others it was left in the fields to be used as manure to enrich the soil.'* The Abbey proclaimed a general fast, and on 9th August all the people of the town and the brethren of the convent processed barefooted from the Abbey to St Mary-in-the-Fields, *'then and there to entreat the Lord and his mother to have pity on the people.'* Given our contemporary concern with changes in weather patterns, it is salutary to read accounts of similar anxieties in the thirteenth century.

Matthew's style

Matthew was not only a collector of information but also a storyteller with a liking for dramatic events. His skill in storytelling lies in his ability to recall a scene and, using vivid language, construct a well paced dialogue to bring it to life. There are numerous examples throughout the Chronicle.

For example, when Henry III confronts the people of Winchester over the lawlessness in the area, Matthew recalls the scene, *'So the lord king had the bailiffs and free men of that county summoned, and addressed them with a grim look, "What is this I hear about you? The complaints of plundered people have reached me, and I have to listen to them. ... How can such things be tolerated any further?" Suddenly the king exclaimed with a fearful shout, "Shut the gates of the castle! Shut them at once."'* The Bishop of Winchester remonstrated with the king, and after he had calmed him down, it was agreed to appoint a jury of twelve men to hear the King's case.

Another example of Matthew's dramatic style is the confrontation between Henry and the Countess of Arundel over her dowry. Matthew writes that after the countess had put her case, *'the king laughed derisively, and curling his nostrils, said, with a raised voice, "What is this, my lady countess? Have the nobles of England agreed with you and given you a charter to be their spokeswoman as you are so eloquent?" To this the countess, although a young woman, replied, "By no means, my lord. Where are the liberties of England, so often granted, so often committed to writing, so often redeemed? I appeal against you before the tribunal of the awful judge of all. May the Lord, the God of vengeance, avenge us." At these words the king was put to shame and silence.'*

Matthew can also be sensitive to a situation, as he is when he remembers Henry sailing from Portsmouth to fight for his possessions in Gascony, leaving his small son standing on the beach. Matthew says *'The boy, Edward, after his father had kissed and wept over him at parting, stood crying and sobbing on the shore, and would not depart as long as he could see the swelling sails of the ships.'*

Matthew's written output: his attitudes and views

Part of the interest in Matthew's Chronicle for anyone wanting a contemporary insight into the twelfth and thirteenth centuries lies in his views about the people he met and his attitude toward the events he witnessed. Matthew has been criticised for his views. Richard Vaughan, in his account of Matthew's writings published in 1984, said *'the*

Chronica Majora is a colourful subjective account of current events rather than a sober history.' But today Matthew's work is valued because it is a personal account and claims to give us, not only Matthew's view, but also the popular view of those around him. His Chronicle is more a political and social commentary than a carefully researched analysis of the thirteenth century. So it is worth considering what he actually said about the people and events he included in his Chronicle.

Matthew seems to have known Henry III (1216-1272) well. The king was interested in Matthew's work, and encouraged him to write up the events he witnessed. For example, in October 1247 Matthew was present in Westminster to witness Henry processing from St Paul's to Westminster Abbey, carrying a crystal container of the Holy Blood. Matthew describes how Henry prepared the night before, *'fasting on bread and water,'* and how he walked on foot, *'wearing a humble dress consisting of a simple cloak, ignoring the rough and uneven road, and only supported by two assistants'*. The monks of Westminster and all the nobility and clergy came out to meet the king; and in his enthusiasm the king not only processed round the Abbey, but also round his palace and his own rooms, before placing the relic in the shrine of St Edward the Confessor. After the proceedings Matthew tells us that Henry noticed him, and *'called him to him, and told him to sit on the steps between the throne and the floor of the church.'* And then said, *'I entreat you ... to write a clear and detailed account of all these proceedings.... so that their memory cannot on any account be lost to posterity ... and he invited the person to whom he said this to dinner with his three companions'*.

Matthew portrays Henry as a devout, family centred king, and he clearly enjoyed his conversations with him later in his life. In 1257 Henry stayed at the Abbey for a week, praying at the shrines of SS Alban and Amphibalus, making offerings of jewellery and silk cloth, one of which was to cover the tombs of the hermits Roger and Sigard in the south aisle. Matthew tells us that he was the king's *'constant companion in the palace, at table, and in his chamber.'* He records the names of the kings and baronies of England *'which Henry recited to him in one of their conversations.'*

Fig. 8: Henry III in procession with the Holy Blood at Westminster Abbey.

Matthew was honoured by the king's recognition of him. But he also recognised the king's weaknesses so that his friendship did not prevent him from being critical of Henry for being over generous to his relatives, for his outbursts of anger, and his failure to manage the English barons for the good of the kingdom. The king needed to have a good understanding with his barons in order to finance the affairs of state, taxation being no more popular then than now. When the relationship broke down, all Henry could do was to plead for aid, or seize resources when there was an opportunity.

Because Henry could not command respect, he resorted to tyrannical outbursts of anger. Matthew commented on an argument between the king and the Bishop of Lincoln in this way: *'the king was as it were carried away by his fury; and not being able to contain his anger, he drove all those who were in his room away from him like a madman.'*

To ask whether Matthew was right in his judgement of Henry, or whether he understood the complexity of royal government, is perhaps to miss the point; what he recorded was both his own view and the view of those around him.

Matthew's ambivalence is evident in his portrayal of other leading characters of his time. He regularly accuses the papacy of greed and duplicity, but at the same time recognises the spiritual authority of the pope's office in protecting the Church. When Frederick II is harshly criticised by Cardinal Reiner, Matthew points out that the force of the criticism is muted by the *'fact that the papalists, enemies of this same Frederick, were defiled with avarice, simony, usury and other vices.'*

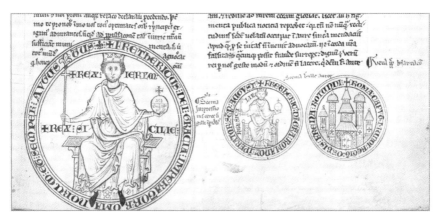

Fig. 9: The seal of Frederick II.

Likewise Matthew is ambivalent towards Frederick II himself. He approved of Frederick's strength of character and decisive leadership, especially when compared to Henry III. He supported Frederick's confrontation with the papacy because it matched his own dislike of papal interference; nevertheless, he had reservations about Frederick's uncompromising attitude towards those who opposed him.

By contrast King Louis IX of France is usually presented as saintly and courageous. When Louis takes the cross his mother and his courtiers are highly critical. But when Louis persists Matthew commends him and comments, *'When those present saw this they recognised that the hand of God was here.'*

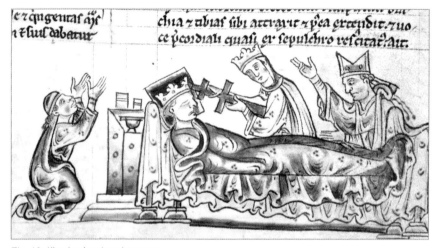

Fig. 10: King Louis takes the cross.

There are many instances where Matthew's view of an individual or situation is vividly and dramatically expressed, where he balances the good with the bad. In his account of Louis IX's Crusade, Matthew portrays William Longspee as the heroic English knight in contrast to the bombastic Count of Artois to typify the cultural differences between the French and English. When the Bishop of Lincoln seeks to exercise episcopal control over St Albans he is to be resisted, but the Bishop is justified in his opposition to papal misuse of patronage. And the Bishops of Durham are generally to be resisted when they interfere with the privileges granted to the Priory of Tynemouth, but at other times are recognised as the authority in pastoral matters. The barons of England are favourably portrayed because they wanted to limit the power of the king and enforce the provisions of Magna Carta. So William Marshall who protected the young Henry III, and Simon de Montfort, the great advocate of representation in exchange for taxation, get favourable mention in the Chronicle: but John Mansel, Henry's chief counsellor, is strongly criticised because he trespasses on the Abbey's privileges. There are many thumbnail sketches of the people and places Matthew came in contact with. Some are noted for the record, many are powerfully presented.

Alternative versions of the Chronicle

The *Chronica Majora* was Matthew's chief work. Matthew's decision to end his Chronicle in 1250, the year he believed the world would end, gave an apocalyptic tone to his writing, and accounts for the didactic and moralistic approach to his material.

Around that time Matthew seems to have decided two things: first, to go through what he had written and remove the comments he thought might offend his readers; secondly to produce a shorter version of the Chronicle.

There is no indication that Matthew had received any adverse reaction to his work: his decision on both accounts seems to have been a personal one. It is possible that, as he grew older and got to know the king and the processes of government better, he felt his judgements had been too harsh. He may have reacted to the passing of the millennial moment by deciding to disseminate the message of the chronicle more widely before he died and to tone down his comments. There is no indication that the full Chronicle was ever a popular read, nor indeed whether it was communicated in any way at all. For whatever reason around 1250 Matthew produced, first *Historia Anglorum* (The History of the English) and *Flores Historiarum* (The Flowers of History) both abridgements of the full Chronicle, and then *Abbrevatio Chronicorum* (A Summary of the Chronicles) which was a shorter version of *Historia*. Around this time he also put together a book of documents which up to then he had copied into the *Chronica Majora*, but which were now overwhelming that work. He called this new manuscript the *Liber Additamentorum* (The Book of Additions). The purpose of the abridgements is not clear; Matthew removed much original material, but he also added new information. None of the abridgements has a clearly differentiated focus to the original Nevertheless, one of the versions, *Flores Historiarum*, was taken up and used by other communities as the basis for their own chronicles. There are 19 extant copies of the *Flores* from the fourteenth century alone, and it became as Vaughan says, *'one of the most popular history books of the age.'*

The 'Gesta Abbatum': Matthew's domestic history

The *Gesta Abbatum* (Deeds of the Abbots) is Matthew's domestic history of the Benedictine community in St Albans. As such, it differs from the broad, national and European focus of the *Chronica Majora*.

Essentially it is an account of the actions taken by the twenty three abbots who ruled the St Albans community between 793 and 1260 (see list on inside cover). It is, however, more than that: it is an account of the foundation of the community, and the subsequent interaction between the monks and their abbot, and between the abbot and the wider world. That wider world consisted of many different interest groups. First and foremost there were the king and the barons who gave land to St Albans; then the pope and the curia in Rome with whom St Albans had an exclusive relationship; followed by the bishops and clergy in England who exercised priestly functions in the community; and there were also the large number of skilled craftsmen who maintained the buildings and beautified the Abbey; those who farmed the manors from which the Abbey derived its food and income; and those who serviced the community and lived in St Albans itself. Finally there was the steady stream of pilgrims who came to the Abbey to venerate St Alban and be healed in some way. It is an interesting account of a small, intense and complex world.

Fig. 11: A monk carrying a crucifix.

As with the chronicle Matthew had a purpose in writing the *Gesta*. He prefaces his manuscript with these words: *'Here are recorded the names of the abbots of the church of St Alban, many of whom made by their own efforts numerous gains in possessions, dignities, sacred vessels and ornaments and constructed many buildings. ... In this way* [that is in recording them in the Gesta] *neither their good works nor indeed their bad ones will perish.'* Matthew had a moral and ascetic message for the abbot and his companions about the way the community should be governed. One element in that message was the power of the abbot and the limits which might be placed on his power. The abbot like the king could become a tyrant. That tendency, Matthew believed, could only be checked by the acceptance of a charter, giving each member of the community the right to have his voice heard and not to be ruled arbitrarily by the will of the abbot. This, however, proved as difficult to achieve in the community as it was in the kingdom.

Date and Sources of the 'Gesta'.

To appreciate the *Gesta* it helps to know when it was written, and where Matthew got his material from. For the lives of the earliest abbots Matthew appears to have relied on an account written by a monk named Bartholomew for Adam the Cellarer who died in 1170, and who did much to consolidate St Albans' power and influence. For the lives of the abbots who lived between 1170 and 1214, Matthew probably used the recollections of the older members of the community who were alive when he was writing his account. Matthew himself knew from personal experience at least two of the abbots whose lives he recorded: William of Trumpington who became abbot in 1214, and John of Hertford who became abbot in 1235. Matthew finished writing his account of the abbots in 1235, and added his account of the election of John of Hertford around 1255.

The Subject Matter of the 'Gesta'.

In the first part of the *Gesta*, from 793 to 1170, Matthew describes the foundation of the monastery in St Albans by Offa, king of Mercia, and its subsequent development. The history of the foundation of the Abbey was as important to Matthew as his belief in the living presence of Alban in his shrine. Matthew measured the success or failure of each abbot by the degree to which he maintained the estates of the Abbey and advanced the cult of Alban, and the building which housed him.

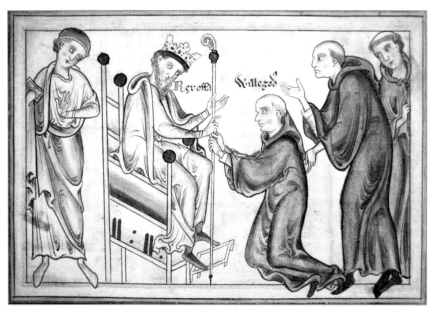

Fig. 12: King Offa invests Willegod as first Abbot.

Having described the foundation of the Abbey, Matthew then proceeds to describe the life of each abbot. One of Matthew's concerns in the first part of the *Gesta* is to counter the claims made by the monks of Odense in Denmark, and by the monks of Ely, to possess the true relics of St Alban. This may seem trivial to us, but it mattered because the authenticity of Alban's presence was the life blood of the community at St Albans. It was this that gave the Abbey its distinction and kept the pilgrims and powerful donors committed. It was critically important to ensure no other community could claim St Alban, and that the cult and the healings associated with it were not compromised. The same concern lay behind the efforts made to develop the cult of St Alban when the martyrdom of Thomas Becket in Canterbury threatened to eclipse all other cults.

In his account of the early history of the Abbey Matthew describes the development of the town of St Albans to the north of the Abbey precincts. Wulsin and the abbots who succeeded him from 950 onwards purchased the fish pool, took possession of Kingsbury manor and removed the building material which could be used to repair the Abbey church from the remains of the Roman city.

It is, however, difficult to confirm Matthew's account of the early abbots because there are no reliable records, partly because of the disruption caused by the Viking wars, but also because Paul de Caen, the first Norman abbot, did not value the pre-Conquest history of the Abbey, and created a decisive break between the Anglo-Saxon and Norman periods. Fortunately, however, there are a number of charters relating to St Albans from the late Anglo-Saxon period, recently edited by Julia Crick, which imply that the community was given a new lease of life around 990. Charters in favour of St Albans were granted by King Aethelred in 996 and 1005; they restored the land and liberties said to have been granted by Offa to St Albans. Their authenticity is open to question, but they suggest that there was a well recognised community in St Albans before the Conquest.

The Abbots of St Albans, 1077-1195

The story of the Abbey in Matthew's day, however, really begins with the Norman Conquest. The *Gesta* records how Abbot Frederick, a supporter of the English nobility, tangled with William the Conqueror. It was Frederick who administered the oath which William swore before Archbishop Lanfranc *'to keep without violation the good and approved ancient laws of the kingdom.'* Frederick spoke out against William's treatment of the English, until William threatened him and St Albans with the loss of their privileges, whereupon Frederick fled to Ely where he died. In his place Lanfranc nominated Paul de Caen, a relative of his, whom William confirmed as abbot in 1077.

It is Paul de Caen, the first Norman abbot, whom Matthew believed set St Albans on the road to success in the post Conquest period. Paul undertook the rebuilding of the Abbey using materials previously gathered from the Roman town of Verulamium, the ruins of which lay in the valley below the Abbey. He repossessed the lands lost during the Conquest, acquired new manors, and established the Priories at Tynemouth, Binham, Hertford and Hatfield. He also set up the scriptorium and donated a library of books to the Abbey. Matthew rated Paul highly, but was critical of his treatment of the Abbey's early history, writing that *'Abbot Paul destroyed the tombs of the noble abbots, his predecessors, whom he was accustomed to call barbarians and bumpkins, either despising them because they were English, or envying them because they had almost all been born of royal stock ...'* Matthew, unlike Paul, valued the history and royal connections of the Abbey, and wanted to emphasise their importance to his contemporaries.

Paul was succeeded by a number of abbots, all of whom contributed to the growing reputation of the Abbey. Of these, Geoffrey de Gorham (1097 – 1119) is one of the most notable. Geoffrey, a teacher from Maine in Normandy, was appointed to run a school in Dunstable. He used drama as a teaching aid and borrowed vestments from the Abbey when presenting a play about St Katherine. Unfortunately his house caught fire and the vestments and his books were burnt. In reparation he became a monk at the Abbey and subsequently rose to be the abbot. He rebuilt the shrine and made it a feature of the Abbey. He established a nunnery at Sopwell and a leprosarium at St Julians. Most notably he supported Christina of Markyate, a religious recluse who established a priory locally. His relationship with Christina seems to have caused criticism in the community. Matthew himself makes no reference to her in the *Gesta*: the account we have was added by Thomas Walsingham in the fifteenth century.

The next significant abbacy is that of Robert de Gorham, a relative of Geoffrey, who was abbot from 1151 to 1167. During Robert's abbacy, Nicholas Breakspear was elected to the papacy in 1154, as Pope Adrian IV. Robert made the most of the connection. Despite the fact that Nicholas had been refused entry to the community at St Albans when young, and remembered the rejection, as pope he issued two bulls making St Albans directly responsible to the papacy. These privileges elevated St Albans to be the premier Abbey in England, a claim which caused some criticism, but which laid the foundation for future success.

During Robert's abbacy Adam the Cellarer was active in the Abbey. He ensured that a number of important land disputes were settled to the Abbey's advantage: the manor of Luton was granted to St Albans; controversies over the relationship with Lincoln diocese were settled; the wood at Northaw was retained; and a dispute with the Earl of Arundel over Wymondham was resolved. All this is recorded in great detail in the *Gesta* as though by an eye witness. The standing of Adam is reflected by the fact that he was buried in the Chapter House along with former abbots in recognition of his achievements, which was an exceptional honour. Even today his remains lie in the Presbytery of the Abbey, along with those of the abbots exhumed when the modern chapter house was built.

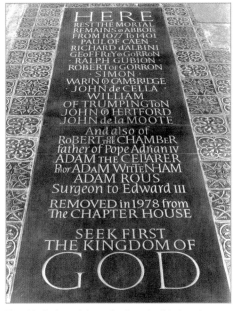

Fig. 13: A slate slab marks the reburial site of some medieval Abbots and monastic officials.

The abbots who succeeded Robert are briefly accounted for: Simon (1167 – 1183) supported Thomas Becket in his disputes with Henry II, but then ensured that the shrine of St Alban maintained its position as Becket's shrine at Canterbury rose to prominence. Warin (1183 – 1195), much liked by Henry II, established the community at St Mary de Pre and developed the cult of St Amphibalus.

Abbots contemporary with Matthew: John de Cella

With the death of Warin in 1195, Matthew begins to record events which fell within his own lifetime or that of his contemporaries. There were three abbots about whom Matthew had reliable knowledge: John de Cella, William of Trumpington, and John of Hertford.

The abbacy of John de Cella ran from 1195 to 1214. Whether Matthew had direct contact with him depends on whether Matthew was involved with the Abbey before he was clothed there as a novice in 1217. Whatever the circumstances, Matthew would have known monks in the community who had known him. Matthew's account of John's abbacy is interesting because it covers a critical period in English history: the struggle between the barons and King John to limit the king's powers, which concluded with the sealing of *Magna Carta* in 1215. In the *Gesta* we can see how that conflict affected the life of St Albans.

In the disturbances of King John's reign the Abbey experienced both the frustrations of the king and the opportunism of the barons. In 1208, King John and England were put under an interdict by Pope Innocent III which closed down the sacramental life of the nation. During this time the king came to St Albans and required the abbot to celebrate divine service for him, which was strictly forbidden by the terms of the interdict. Abbot John refused, and incurred the king's anger until he paid a fine to release the Abbey from the king's control. Subsequently the Abbey paid large sums of money to both the king and his adversaries to retain its privileges and possessions.

Nevertheless, during those troubled times the Abbey was a safe refuge and many men applied to enter the religious life. Matthew records that Abbot John limited the number of professed monks to 100. But such great numbers put pressure on the facilities and management of the Abbey. One solution to the problem of numbers was to move members of the community away from St Albans to the various priories managed by the Abbey. This, however, was an unpopular process because it isolated the monk from the mother house, and resistance to it was strong.

It was during Abbot John's time that an extension to the west end of the Abbey was started. The process was disastrous. Abbot John was not a forceful manager and was, as Matthew says, *'ignorant of everyday affairs after the fashion of scholars.'* The first attempt collapsed, and subsequently took 27 years to complete. Matthew comments, *'that unfortunate building work absorbed everything as the sea does rivers, and still made no progress.'* Abbot John was more successful in rebuilding the refectory and dormitory of the monks, with the new ones *'perfectly and blamelessly finished.'* The Abbot also encouraged Walter of Colchester, whom Matthew describes as *'an incomparable painter and sculptor,'* and his assistants to enhance the ornamentation of the church. It was at this time that some of the wall paintings which can still be seen in the Abbey were commenced. The programme of decoration was continued by the next Abbot, William of Trumpington. William also completed the west end, re-roofed the tower, reinforced the transepts, and glazed most of the windows.

Nevertheless despite the difficulties Abbot John experienced, Matthew commends him as *'distinguished by his holiness and religion ... leaving his Abbey in as good a state as the times would allow.'* Abbot John personified the message that Matthew wanted to communicate to his contemporaries: the need for courage and commitment in following the Rule, and in maintaining the status of the Abbey under all circumstances.

Fig. 14: An early wall painting in the Nave, c. 1200-1225

William of Trumpington

For Matthew the abbot who best fitted his belief in the need for strong leadership was the one under whom he served his early years in the community: this was William of Trumpington, abbot from 1214 to 1235, whose time in charge was as fraught with problems as his predecessor's. He was elected to the abbacy just before the king was forced to seal *Magna Carta*. When it became clear that the king did not intend to honour the charter, the barons rebelled and civil war broke out. Like his predecessor he then had to defend the Abbey and hold the community together. Wisely William refused to renounce his allegiance to the king as the rebels demanded, and when John died and his son Henry inherited the kingdom, the abbot had the support of the young king and his council. William, however, was a forceful character. Initially he fell out with those in the community who had elected him, but, calling in the Papal Legate, he quelled the opposition. He renounced the charter which he had helped to draw up at the end of John de Cella's abbacy, which sought to ban the practice of exiling monks to distant priories against their will.

Matthew dramatises the start of William's rule in a confrontation with the monastic chapter. William is accused of cynically abandoning his former commitments. Matthew describes the scene: *'The abbot gnashing his teeth .. and with the colour of his* face changed and his whole body bent and quivering, replied "It is true that I drew up the charter you are referring to ...but I did not appreciate what I was doing. For that reason I can undo what I have done, and what has been confirmed by me can be annulled by me. The things I formerly believed in stand no longer, for I know now what I didn't know before." On this Dom Amalric muttered under his breath "That's true for now you know you are the abbot, which you didn't before." The abbot heard this and was not pleased.'

As soon as peace came William set out to visit all the priories linked to St Albans 'to reform whatever needed reformation,' and replace the priors who did not live up to his standards with new appointees. Matthew wrote: 'I think it worth recording ... that this abbot prudently calmed down every schismatic tumult ... and reduced everyone to his beck and call so that none dared to murmur against him.'

The rest of Matthew's account of William's abbacy is taken up with the renovations and ornamentation of the Abbey for which William was responsible. At the end of his account Matthew attaches a paper detailing the cost to the Abbey of the civil war in the payment of bribes and the replacement of requisitioned goods. It is a staggering sum, equivalent to nine years of the Abbey's regular annual income.

John of Hertford

From his account of the death of William in 1235 onwards, Matthew seems to change his objective in writing the history of the Abbey. In his account of John of Hertford's abbacy Matthew describes first of all the order for an abbatial funeral, and then the process of appointing and installing a new abbot. Why this change? Matthew explains that the Lateran Council of 1215 had created new rules for the appointment of abbots, and that, because it was twenty years since St Albans had made such an appointment, it was 'hardly surprising that everyone was uncertain how to proceed.' Consequently the senior monks took advice, and Matthew was asked 'to place the progress of affairs on permanent written record.' He then sets out the procedure for the election of a new abbot, not only describing the process, but also recording for future reference the legal declarations to accompany it. He notes that the procedure followed at St Albans was commended by the pope and cardinals in Rome. This is as far as Matthew takes his account of the lives of the abbots in the *Gesta*. Subsequent events affecting the life of the St Albans' community during the abbacy of John of Hertford are recorded in the *Chronica Majora.*

The *Gesta Abbatum*, alongside the *Chronica Majora,* is the most complete record we have of life in a large religious community in the thirteenth century. It gives us an intriguing insight into the sensitivities of its members, and in particular of Matthew himself. Matthew may have been prejudiced and oversensitive, inconsistent and confused by what was going on around him, but we cannot get closer to the reality of the thirteenth century than through his account.

Matthew's Lives of the Saints

In addition to writing the *Chronica Majora* and the domestic history of his house, Matthew also wrote five lives of saints (often called hagiographies): SS. Alban and Amphibalus, St Thomas Becket, St Edmund of Abingdon, St Edward the Confessor, and a life of Stephen Langton, Archbishop of Canterbury. To these we should perhaps add *The Lives of the Two Offas* which describes the rediscovery of the remains of St Alban and the foundation of the Abbey in the eighth century.

Fig. 15: King Offa and his men discover Alban's tomb

Of these lives four are written in French verse, and two in Latin prose. We may wonder why Matthew decided to write the majority of his lives in French verse when the bulk of his work was written in Latin. What was his intention, and for whom did he write them? His *Chronica* and the *Gesta* were written, as far as we can tell, as historical records for the community in St Albans, in line with the practice in other religious houses of the time. But for whom would Matthew have produced saints' lives in French verse? The answer may lie in the dedication of his *Life of St Edward* and in notes Matthew wrote in his manuscript of the *Life of St Alban*.

The readership

In the opening stanzas of the *Life of St Edward*, Matthew dedicates his work to Eleanor, the wife of Henry III. He explains that although he is writing in French for her, there is a Latin version which gives authority to what he has written. Matthew writes, '*Noble, well-born lady, Eleanor, rich queen of England ...I who have prepared this book for you put it in your care.'* Matthew assumed the Queen would be interested in St Edward the Confessor because Henry was devoted to his memory and rebuilt Westminster Abbey to enshrine Edward's remains. But there was also a group of noblewomen in Henry's court for whom these lives were written. On a fly-leaf in the manuscript of the *Life of St Alban* there is a note in Matthew's hand, asking that the manuscript should be sent to the Countess of Arundel and that she should send it on to the Countess of Cornwall together with Matthew's *Life of St Thomas Becket*. As Jocelyn Wogan-Browne says in her introduction to the *Life of St Alban*, *'Noblewomen were the audiences for Paris's saints' lives and integral to the dissemination and practice of St Alban's cult.'*

The Intention

What was Matthew's intention in writing saints' lives? A saint's life is an account of the actions and suffering of an individual in witnessing to their faith. In the early church the saint was initially recognised by the bishop at a local level, and then occasionally incorporated into the universal calendar of the church. From the twelfth century onwards the papacy sought to regularise this process. By the beginning of the thirteenth century canonisation had become the exclusive right of the papacy, and a system to justify this privileged status was introduced.

The lives which Matthew wrote were in line with this development. A life was not a biography as we might understand it, although it would set out the historical facts as far as they were known. The saint's life concentrated on the deeds of the individual and in particular itemised the miracles worked by the saint. These claims were tested by the papacy by interviewing witnesses to judge their credibility. We can see this process at work in Matthew's *Life of St Edmund*. Matthew sets out the known facts about Edmund's family and his career, highlighting his virtues: his abstinence, devotion to prayer and conformity to the will of God. Matthew supports his account by including the testimonies submitted to Rome by Walter, Archbishop of York, and Roger Bacon, a Dominican Friar from Oxford. In the case of the other saints whose lives Matthew wrote, he uses accounts which had been recognised by the church, and which Matthew accepted as authoritative.

There is, however, another dimension to Matthew's saints' lives; that is a quasi-political sub-text which Matthew wished to convey. In each of his lives Matthew ensures that his criticism of contemporary events is aired; the corruption of the papal curia, the failure of the king to promote native born Englishmen, the excessive expenditure of the court, and the many other grievances of Matthew's time, are here expressed anachronistically.

So for example, St Edward the Confessor is portrayed by Matthew as the ideal king of England, the last of the Anglo-Saxon kings before the Conquest, who promoted native born Englishmen and rejected luxury, both policies that Matthew wished Henry to adopt. Matthew wanted Henry to see himself as the legitimate heir to a particular style of kingship and to follow his ancestor's example. Matthew dedicated the Life to Queen Eleanor, not only because he respected her, but also because he hoped she would encourage Henry to make that commitment.

Likewise in his lives of St Edmund, Thomas Becket and Stephen Langton, the sub-text is about the long running struggle to make the church independent of the state, and free from royal interference. The church consequently had to confront the power of the state and the papacy. As a result Edmund goes into exile and goes to Pontigny as Thomas Becket and Stephen Langton had done before him. Matthew's message is that despite the opening paragraphs of *Magna Carta*, the church was still not free. The themes of his Chronicle and the *Gesta* are repeated in Matthew's lives of the saints.

How important were the saints' lives to Matthew? The modern historian may find the Chronicle and the *Gesta* a more fertile hunting ground for an account of thirteenth century life, but for Matthew the writing of a saint's Life was probably higher in his order of priorities. C.H.Lawrence in his study of Matthew Paris's *Life of St Edmund* said, *'the cultus of the saints was a theme which called for his best efforts. Matthew worked as assiduously in this field as in the other.'* Matthew's saints' lives also give us an insight into Matthew's network of friendships and his links with the royal court: in these works he is less the austere ascetic more the courtier monk. After this we may ask again, just who was Matthew Paris?

The Art of Matthew Paris

Matthew's artistic style and its development

Fig. 16: The elevation of Alban's relics.

Later medieval chroniclers praise Matthew's artistic skills. As far as we know he was self-taught. His approach to his writings was strongly visual; his descriptions are lively and often detailed, and this approach is mirrored in his illustrative work. It appears that he had a natural talent which he fostered without the instruction of a current master of the trade. As a result his work is a mixture of experiment and invention carried out in often archaic styles.

It seems that the heyday of artistic book production at St Albans Abbey, which had produced such works as the St Albans Psalter in the twelfth century, was over by the time Matthew became a monk. However, the Abbey's library contained a wide selection of books, some of which would have been illustrated. Moreover the enhancement of the Abbey church was given new impetus when Abbot William of Trumpington finally finished the west end work which had dragged on for so long. Matthew refers frequently in the *Gesta* to the work of Brother Walter of Colchester, a fellow monk, who was an artist, sculptor and metalworker. While it is tempting to think that some of the illustrations in Matthew's work allow us to make a tentative reconstruction of the decorative work of the Abbey at this time, there is no foundation for this.

Matthew travelled a lot, sometimes to and with the court. We can assume that he saw many works of art and manuscripts in palaces and churches such as Canterbury, Winchester, Peterborough, St Edmundsbury and Westminster. Perhaps he even kept a pattern book or portfolio of drawings of works he had seen.

Matthew is careful in his drawing. Illustrations are carefully drawn in lead point prior to the use of ink and finally colour washed. This was a popular style in Anglo-Saxon art prior to the Norman Conquest His outlines are clear and definite with lighter linear detail on draperies although he is perhaps overly fond of putting patterns on these which can appear somewhat busy and fussy. Initially he tends to cling to the earlier way of using the colour wash as light tinting along lines, developing it much later to the gothic way of using wider expanses of colour or to highlight salient features (fig. 7 and fig. 10) Yet he abandons the Anglo Saxon and Romanesque treatment of drapery for an emergent gothic style where the folds are no longer stylized into damp fold patterns but fall in smaller multiple more realistic folds (fig. 16). In short while the medium refers back to Anglo Saxon times, the execution is more in the transitional style of late Romanesque and early Gothic, while the content is of his day.

The figures of his mature style, shown in a variety of poses and profiles, display different facial features and expressions. They have relatively large heads and the graceful bodies typical of the early gothic period. Hands and arms are drawn so as to indicate not only action but also intention and emotion (fig. 16).

As was common at the time little interest is shown in landscape and background with one exception: the sea. Matthew refers frequently to the sea, often using water as a metaphor for money. It appears in many forms in his illustrations. Always green it is shown flat, stormy or undulating (fig. 7).

Matthew does not restrict himself to the traditional colour wash palette of earth colours but expands this to include bright reds and blues which he frequently uses in the rubrics as well as in his illustrative work (fig. 8 and fig. 16).

Matthew makes a clear distinction between what could be styled formal and informal art work. All formal illustrations have a double frame and have usually been executed on a separate piece of vellum stuck into the relevant space. Perhaps this is a reflection of his need to be sure that this work was as high quality as it could be. More formal illustrations appear occasionally in the two versions of the *Chronica Majora* but far more importantly in the *Life of St Alban*.

Fig. 17: Veronica's veil.

Matthew's drawing of the Veronica (fig. 17) is one of the first depictions of its kind. It is in full colour, frontal and almost Byzantine in composition. Another image of the Veronica in the *Chronica Majora* is also framed, with a space deliberately left for it in the text.

The portraits of enthroned kings in the *Historia Anglorum* and the *Abbreviatio Chronicorum* are set four to a page each within a border and each king under his own architectural device.

Fig. 18: Kings of England.

By the 1250s, perhaps due to advancing years or failing sight, Matthew appears somewhat less interested in illustration and the style becomes heavier. Yet it is possibly from this period that we find in the *Chronica Majora* the mature skilled illustrations of the procession of the Holy Blood (fig. 8) and the murder of Thomas Becket (fig. 19).

Fig. 19: The murder of Thomas Becket.

An eye for detail

Matthew broke fresh ground in his depiction of heraldic shields. We have no evidence of coats of arms prior to 1195 and yet there are 193 in the manuscript of the *Chronica Majora* in Corpus Christi College, Cambridge, most of them in the margins marking where Matthew mentions the owner of the device (fig. 2). This is the first known medieval collection of depictions of coats of arms. We find others in the *Liber Additamentorum* including a full page of 42. Perhaps this knowledge comes from his familiarity with the court or from the Abbey's distinguished visitors.

A desire to set out knowledge diagrammatically influenced chroniclers, including Matthew. He includes a family tree of the pre-Conquest kings of England as well as tables and diagrams for calculating the moveable date of Easter.

As shown in his depiction of heraldic devices Matthew is keen to incorporate accurate detail into his drawings. While he has little awareness of historical accuracy and his Roman soldiers wear medieval armour (fig. 25), we are struck by the amount of detail in his illustrations of contemporary events. He took great care in the accurate reproduction of the seal of the Emperor Frederick II (fig. 9) as well as a coin of the period. In his drawings of the siege of Damietta both the siege and the warship (fig. 7) are drawn with great attention to detail as is the armour.

Fig. 20: Parade in Cremona.

The elephant carrying the Cremona band in the *Chronica Majora* has no knees. But once Matthew has seen the elephant kept in the Tower of London (see front cover) he has placed the knees accurately low on the legs, the trunk is well observed and the elephant colour washed in grey. On the other hand, from the balloon shaped humps they bear, it is safe to assume that Matthew had had no occasion to meet with a camel (fig. 28). Interestingly for a churchman he appears to have been more observant of castles than churches; even his own Abbey is indistinguishable from other ecclesiastical foundations.

Occasionally we have a sense of playfulness: a pulley is hung on the frame surrounding the drawing of the building of St Alban's Abbey (where thirteenth century tools and methods are used in the building of the eighth century Abbey) and in the reports of an earthquake houses topple off a line of script.

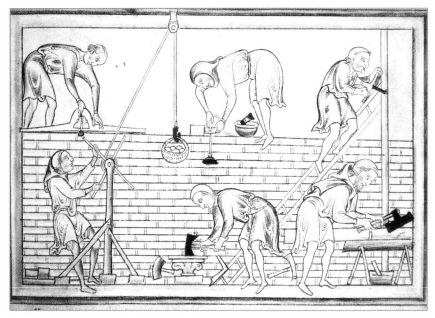

Fig. 21: The building of St Alban's church by King Offa.

The use of illustrations in the 'Chronica Majora'

It is believed that Matthew first started illustrating the *Chronica Majora* in 1236 as he was copying out the work of Roger of Wendover. Here, an unprecedented number of lively, and seemingly ad hoc, illustrations enhance Matthew's accounts of contemporary and past events. They are to be found in the margins and at the foot of many pages.

At the simplest level Matthew uses symbols in the margins in order to cross reference documents copied into the *Liber Additamentorum* with the discussion of the same in the Chronicle itself.

Other images at the sides are usually simple designs and, in similar vein to the cross referencing marks, are used to indicate the account of a specific event. Joined hands surmounted by a crown mark where Matthew describes a royal wedding. A shield indicates an account of the deeds of its owner, upturned it marks their death. King William Rufus's death and its manner are both indicated at the relevant place in the Chronicle (fig. 2).

It appears that the layout of the pages was specially devised to accommodate Matthew's art as the margin at the foot of the page is deeper than one would expect. The often dynamic and dramatic narrative is frequently matched by an animated illustration of the scene, be it Biblical, mythical, historical or contemporary. Often these are accompanied by a caption, extra text, or a scroll. Important events such as the Council of Lyons or the murder of Becket (fig. 19) sometimes have a more static and monumental appearance. Unfortunately for the reader this space at the foot of every page does not always contain an illustration.

Fig. 22: The meeting of the pope and prelates at the Council of Lyons.

Artistic development in the 'Chronica Majora'

Although the illustrations of the **Chronica Majora** were not executed in chronological order we can gain an insight into the order of their execution by using stylistic analysis. This enables us to trace the development of his talent in both composition and penmanship.

Gradually we see the development of his ideas about composition. Matthew's early illustrations tend to show several separate figures each in their own space with no obvious relationship to each other. The development of his skills from these disparate figures is shown in some of his later drawings such as the busy interpretation of the Battle of Bouvines where the melée of men and horses matches the immediacy of his description of battle.

Fig. 23: The battle of Bouvines, 1214.

In the sophisticated composition of Henry III carrying the Holy Blood through the streets of London (fig. 8) Matthew uses space to define importance and relationships.

He develops an awareness of the impact of diagonal lines and triangular composition to connect figures which he uses to great effect in the illustration of the death of Alban.

Matthew's figure style varies dramatically. Initially he drew small stocky people. These busy figures often form rhythmic patterns as in the illustration of the siege of Damietta (fig. 7).   Heads are shown in profile and all have similar expressions: blunt noses, furrowed brows and down-turned mouths are common to many of them. As Matthew's confidence and penmanship developed the figures, such as those of the death of Becket or the Council of Lyons (fig. 19 and fig. 22), are more monumental, with poses, profiles and facial expressions much more varied. Draperies become expressive and agitated with fluttering flowing lines.

Fig. 24: The martyrdom of Alban from the *Chronica Majora.*

The Life of St Alban

Probably begun in the mid-1240s, the *Life of St Alban* features Matthew's mature style. It seems that Matthew worked first of all on the illustrations for this book and that they predate the text.

On each page of the *Life* is an illustration of the textual account on that page. Matthew lends to these illustrations a new gravitas with their double frames and their prominent position on the page. The illustrations were each done on a separate piece of vellum

Fig. 25: The martyrdom of Alban, from the *Life of St Alban.*

which was then stuck in to the book. In contrast to the immediacy of many of the illustrations of the *Chronica Majora* they tend to be more static. It is in this work that we first come across the Alban cross which Matthew uses repeatedly in the hands of Alban or Amphibalus. As in the *St Albans Psalter* feet break into the frames, not with flamboyance and defiance but just enough to liberate the composition. In the later pages, Matthew has begun to use a little gold leaf. It is, however, sparse and used to pick out details such as crowns and halos. Somehow his style leads us to believe that less is more.

The illustrations of the *Life* are well balanced; the people are placed in coherent groupings and the action and emphasis are clear. In short they are the mature, confident expression of his art used in the service of the cult at the centre of his life.

Unlike the illustrations in the *Chronica Majora* they appear to have been done in the order we see them. The compositions become denser with figures which have a certain monumentality, suitable for the events they recount. Even within this work, perhaps the pinnacle of his artistic achievement, we can see Matthew's style develop.

The early illustrations are carefully executed with emphatic smooth outlines and patterned details. Proportions are normal, movements restricted, and facial features small. Later illustrations are more densely packed with figures with a variety of facial expressions. They have larger heads which are sometimes somewhat distorted in order to express emotions and character, especially in villains. The final illustrations show monumental figures with large expressive heads, complex drapery and crisper more delicate lines.

The Maps of Matthew Paris

Matthew Paris has left us an unprecedented series of coloured maps. Very different from earlier examples, these already exhibit some of the features we associate with modern-day maps and demonstrate a break with earlier conventions. The most common type of map in Matthew's time was the *Mappa Mundi*, such as that of Hereford. Usually this was a diagrammatic representation of encyclopaedic knowledge of the world - a world with Jerusalem at its centre - rather than an attempt at geographical accuracy. Some of these, including the one at Westminster, were known to Matthew and indeed he names the ones he used as a source for his own attempt at this genre. However his one surviving attempt is cursory and displays little of the plethora of pictorial information we expect.

Matthew, it appears, was interested in something a little more realistic. While lacking the careful attention to detail, scale and relevant position of features which we expect in later examples his maps, nonetheless, mark a huge step forward in the history of cartography. The increased accuracy together with the variety of maps he produced makes his work unique in the mid thirteenth century. The maps fall into three distinct categories: the itineraries which are schematized maps of the route from England to Apulia (the place of departure for boats to the Easter Mediterranean), maps of the Holy Land, and finally maps of Great Britain.

As we are aware from Matthew's use of diagram in the genealogies of English kings and his symbols linking entries in the *Chronica Majora* with documents copied into the *Liber Additamentorum*, Matthew is comfortable with the use of diagram and symbol - the basic tools of a cartographer.

The Itineraries

We find four sets of itineraries from St Albans to Apulia. What was the purpose of these long thin itineraries which are laid out two columns to a page? In the twelfth century *Liber Sancti Jacobi* Aimery Picaud tells the pilgrim which route to take on his or her way to Santiago. He tells of the towns to pass through, where to stop and what to see. It is possible that Matthew with his keen visual sense has turned verbal instructions such as these into diagrams and illustrations.

The reader starts at the bottom of the page and reads up the page as though walking towards the horizon. For those used to 'reading' up historiated stained glass windows this would not have been a problem. Having reached the top the reader then repeats the process with the second column. There is no doubt that these maps do show the route accurately enough for the traveller who is able to ask for the road from one place to another to follow them with some degree of success. Towns are viewed as if at eye level and from the viewpoint of the person approaching. For example, London is depicted as the traveller from St Albans would approach it. The cartographic convention of two parallel lines signifying a road is so new as to be explained in French along the route.

The journey is also divided up into sections for one day's walk, although the length of these varies considerably. Topographical features are given little attention and the real obstacles such as the English Channel and the Alps are merely hinted at, usually occurring at the top and bottom of a page.

Initially the route gives little choice as to direction; then, as it proceeds through France, small diversions become possible. The first alternative routes leave the main roads at 45 degree angles: later these angles become more haphazard. These peripheral routes often lead to major religious centres. As the walker heads south in Italy choices of route become ever more evident and there is an option of visiting Rome or even Sicily. These are shown on flaps specially added for the purpose to the main page.

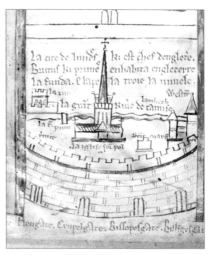

Fig. 26: London as seen when approaching from St Albans.

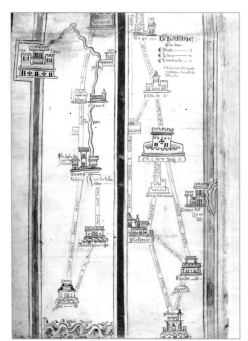

Fig. 27: The Itinerary across Lombardy, from Turin to Reggio Emilia.

We have no information that Matthew undertook the journeys he describes. Indeed the decreasing accuracy as the route leads beyond Paris suggests the opposite. It is possible that the main provider of information for these itinerary maps was Richard, Duke of Cornwall, brother of Henry III and a close friend of Matthew. He had been to the Crusades and had probably used the route depicted, much of which was also used by the traveller to Rome. Perhaps Matthew also received information from visitors to the Abbey who not only brought news of far flung places but also told Matthew how to reach them and had input into his diagrammatic drawings.

The maps do not stand alone: in the copies of the *Chronica Majora* in Corpus Christi College Cambridge and in the British Library they are bound with the Chronicle. This suggests that their intended use was other than a practical aide memoire for the traveller.

This was the great age of pilgrimage. Many people wished to travel to the Holy Land to visit the land of Christ's birth, death and resurrection. But the ultimate goal of the pilgrim was the soul's arrival in the heavenly Jerusalem, not the one at the Eastern end of the Mediterranean.

Enclosed within the cloister, the monk was encouraged to use the restriction of physical movement to enable and support spiritual pilgrimage and travel. In other words the monk contemplating the maps could prayerfully use his imagination and spirituality to make an internal pilgrimage starting and remaining within the cloister. Beginning at the bottom of the page - the part nearest him - the monk, in his mind's eye, would cross the terrain until he reached the horizon at the top of the page then repeat the process. Finally, having arrived in spirit in Apulia, he would take the boat eastwards across the Mediterranean towards Jerusalem.

The Holy Land Maps

Matthew's Holy Land maps return to the convention of placing East at the top of the page. These also display something of the old *mappa mundi* style with the appearance of flora and fauna as well as written accounts of legends and texts of holy places.   We see ships arriving and once again the topographical obstacle has occurred at a page break. It is possible that these maps are a continuation of the route maps showing the final destination. However we are left uncertain as to whether the destination here is the Crusaders' city of Acre or the earthly Jerusalem. Acre, the Crusaders' capital, is shown larger than Jerusalem which appears isolated and unobtainable as it was to the Crusaders. Scenes of the Crusaders' struggles are marked, as are certain biblical sites.   While Jerusalem is depicted as the square city described in the book of Revelation, its situation and size sit ill with its being the ultimate goal of internal or actual pilgrimage.

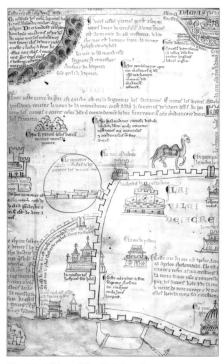

Fig. 28: A Map of the Holy Land.

Fig. 29: A Map of Great Britain.

The maps of England and Scotland, which were probably produced after 1245, are the earliest extant detailed maps. No two are the same suggesting that Matthew was interested enough in cartography to allow his depictions to evolve. The differences suggest that each map was drawn freehand without reference to the others. In comparison with the Holy Land maps there are no accompanying verbal descriptions or accounts. Hadrian's Wall is one of the few details beyond rivers, towns and monasteries to be depicted.

Matthew shows an awareness of scale by his comment on a map of Great Britain that it should have been longer had the page allowed. However not all towns are correctly placed and on one map at least some rivers are indicated simply where they flow through a town. Many of the places marked are monastic sites. There is, as one would expect, far more detail on the English part of the map than the Scottish part.

Flying in the face of convention, Matthew chose to orientate these maps with the north at the top. It is unclear whether this is purely because this orientation is more suited to the shape of the page. In the *Chronica Majora* the map of Britain follows the map of the Holy Land and precedes the genealogy of the English kings. Perhaps all the maps are in some way linked. Suppose the pilgrim, actual or spiritual has followed the route to the Holy Land and then returned to Britain with its venerable monarchy. On his return he will land at Dover then perhaps make his way, up the page, towards the north through St Albans towards Newcastle and the Scottish border.

Conventions

The maps show a consistent use of colour. The sea is green and rivers are blue. Towns are depicted in a series of earth colours. Larger areas are named in red. Places are named in black although Jerusalem is labelled in both red and black.

Matthew's conventional mapping signs, such as the two parallel lines for roads and the crenellations for Hadrian's Wall, are some of the earliest known. There is a mixture of viewpoints: some features such as Jerusalem, being depicted from above while others, animals and ships for example, are depicted as being on eye level. However a glance at a modern OS map will confirm that this 'confusion' still exists today.

Conclusion

Our knowledge of Matthew's origins may be limited but his commitment to recording the events of his time, his criticisms of institutional failure, and his dedication to St Alban and his community, have left us an invaluable picture of society in the thirteenth century. Despite his prejudices and peculiarities, he has left us a wealth of information which is a constant source of interest and enables us to reconstruct the concerns of his contemporaries, and to interpret the main events of his time.

Matthew's illustrations, with their variety of subject matter and approach, enhance and complement his writings. His maps and the record of shields remain fundamental to our knowledge of the development of heraldry and cartography to this day. The reader would indeed be the poorer had Matthew not developed his latent artistic skill.

Matthew died in June 1259. Some attempt was made to continue both the *Chronica* and the *Gesta* but it was not until the end of the fourteenth century when Thomas of Walsingham took up his pen that the great tradition of chronicle writing at St Albans revived.

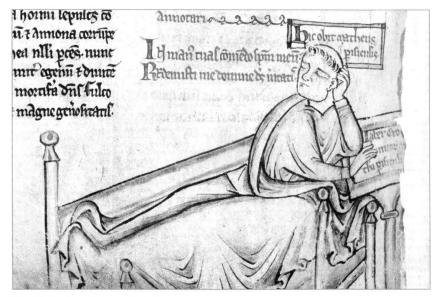

Fig. 30: Matthew Paris on his deathbed.

Acknowledgements:

Michael Clasby would like to thank David Carpenter, Richard Cassidy and Sophie Ambler of Kings College London, and Gail Thomas wishes to thank John McNeill, each of whom made valuable comments.

The Friends of St Albans Abbey are grateful to the Master and Fellows of Corpus Christi College, Cambridge, the Board of Trinity College Dublin and the British Library for permission to reproduce images from their collections.

About the authors:

Michael Clasby has a BA Hons in English Literature and Language from University College London, worked in a local authority in Hertfordshire, and after retirement completed an MA in Medieval History at Kings College London. Gail Thomas has a BA Hons from University College London in French, a diploma from London University in the History of Art and an MA from Birkbeck College in Medieval Studies.

List of illustrations

Front cover: ©Corpus Christi College, Cambridge (CCCC), MS 16, f.ivr.
Inside cover: Abbots of St Albans Abbey, 793 - 1260
Fig. 1: ©The British Library Board (B.Lib.) Cotton MS Nero DVII, f.50v.
Fig. 2: ©CCCC, MS 16, f. 108v.
Fig. 3: B.Lib., Royal 14 CVII, f.123v.
Fig. 4: B.Lib., Royal 14 CVII, f.9
Fig. 5: ©CCCC, MS 16, f. 167r.
Fig. 6: ©CCCC, MS 7, f. 105v.
Fig. 7: ©CCCC, MS 16, F. 059v.
Fig. 8: ©CCCC, MS 16, f. 216r.
Fig. 9: ©CCCC, MS 16, f. 127r.
Fig. 10: ©CCCC, MS 16, f. 183r.
Fig. 11: ©CCCC, MS 16, f. 093v.
Fig. 12: ©Trinity College, Dublin (TCD), MS 177, f.60v.
Fig. 13: ©David Kelsall
Fig. 14: ©Cathedral Archives
Fig. 15: ©TCD, MS 177, f.59r.
Fig. 16: ©TCD, MS 177, f.61r.
Fig. 17: B.Lib., Arundel 157, f.2.
Fig. 18: B.Lib., Royal 14 CVII, f.9
Fig. 19: ©CCCC, MS 26, f. 132r.
Fig. 20: ©CCCC, MS 16, f. 152v.
Fig. 21: ©TCD, MS 177, f.60r.
Fig. 22: B.Lib., Royal 14 CVII, f.138v.
Fig. 23: ©CCCC, MS 16, f. 041r.
Fig. 24: ©CCCC, MS 26, f. 058v.
Fig. 25: ©TCD, MS 177, f.38r.
Fig. 26: B.Lib., Royal 14 CVII, f.2.
Fig. 27: B.Lib., Royal 14 CVII. f.3
Fig. 28: B.Lib., Royal 14 CVII, f.4v.
Fig. 29: B.Lib., Royal 14 CVII, f.5v.
Fig. 30: B.Lib., Royal 14 CVII, f.218v
Fig. 31: ©CCCC, MS 26, f.viir
Back cover: B.Lib., Royal 14 CVII, f.6.

Quotations from Matthew Paris's works are taken from the following translations:
Giles, J.A., *Matthew Paris's English History*, Vols. 1 and 2. London, 1889.
Giles, J.A., *Roger of Wendover's Flowers of History*. London, 1889.
Vaughan, R., *Chronicles of Matthew Paris*, Alan Sutton, 1984
Also from an unpublished translation by David Preest.

Further Reading

Chronicles of Matthew Paris, edited and translated by Richard Vaughan (Alan Sutton, 1984) contains a selection of passages from the *Chronica Majora* and *Gesta Abbatum*; the illustrated version of this book (Alan Sutton, 1993) reproduces some of Matthew's drawings from the autograph Mss at Corpus Christi College, Cambridge.

The Life of St Alban by Matthew Paris, ed. and trans.by Jocelyn Wogan-Browne and Thelma Fenster. Arizona, 2010.

The Life of St Edmund by Matthew Paris, ed. and trans. by C.H. Lawrence. Alan Sutton, 1996.

The Life of St Edward by Matthew Paris, ed. and trans. by Jocelyn Wogan-Browne and Thelma Fenster. Arizona, 2008.

Binski, Paul, *Becket's Crown, Art and Imagination in Gothic England*, Yale, 2004.

Bolton, Brenda and Duggan, Anne (eds), *Adrian IV The English Pope (1154-59)*, Ashgate, 2003.

Carpenter, David , *The Struggle for Mastery, History of Britain, 1066-1284*, Penguin, 2003.

Clanchy, M. T. (ed), *From Memory to Written Record*, 2nd edition, Blackwell, 1993.

Connolly, Daniel K., *The Maps of Matthew Paris*, Boydell, 2009.

Crick, Julia (ed), *Charters of St Alban*, Oxford, 2007.

Gransden, Antonia, *Historical Writing in England c.550-c.1307*, Routledge, 1974.

Harvey, P. D. A., *Medieval Maps*, Brtish Library, 1991.

Lewis, Suzanne, *The Art of Matthew Paris in the Chronica Majora*, California, 1987.

Vaughan, Richard, *Matthew Paris*, Cambridge, 1958.

The Fraternity of the Friends of St Albans Abbey

This book has been published by the Fraternity of the Friends of St Albans Abbey, a medieval organisation which was refounded in 1949 as a registered charity to support and care for this Cathedral and Abbey Church. The Friends include people of all faiths and none. Further details on membership and an application form may be found on the Cathedral website:

www.stalbanscathedral.org/community/friends-of-the-abbey